IMAGES
of Scotland

DUNFERMLINE

The sunshine glints on the tramlines as the Town House dominates this late 1920s view from High Street into Bridge Street.

IMAGES
of Scotland

DUNFERMLINE

George Beattie

TEMPUS

We found him seated in a corner of his favourite bar in the City Hotel—he still calls it the City Arms.

" Goodall's!," he mused, " Aye, they've been going for a wheen o' years . . . I mind o' some of their auld drivers . . . Cabby Robertson, him wha drove the waggonette up to Saline . . . Aye, they were real characters. The auld joke wis that if Goodall's couldna' gie you a sober driver for their phaetons they'd gie you wan you couldna' fill fu'!"

There was a pause as the old man thought back through the years.

" Aye," he continued, " Monie o' auld Goodall's drivers bocht a gill frae Fraser's shop doon the toon. It cost them 6d a gill . . . grand days they were . . . an nae breathalysers . . . And noo, cars restricted . . . aye restricted tae 70 miles an hoor on they motorways."

" Och they've been some awfu' changes. Mon, ye canna get a gill o' the cratur in Fraser's at 6d ony mair."

FRASER & CARMICHAEL

LIMITED

1866 - 1969

congratulate JOHN GOODALL AND CO., LTD. on their Centenary 1869-1969.

Fraser & Carmichael advert.

First published 2001, reprinted 2007

Tempus Publishing Limited
Cirencester Road, Chalford, Stroud, Gloucestershire, GL6 8PE
www.tempus-publishing.com

British Library Cataloguing in Publication Data.
A catalogue record for this book is available from the British Library.

ISBN 978 07524 2127 8
Typesetting and origination by Tempus Publishing Limited.

Contents

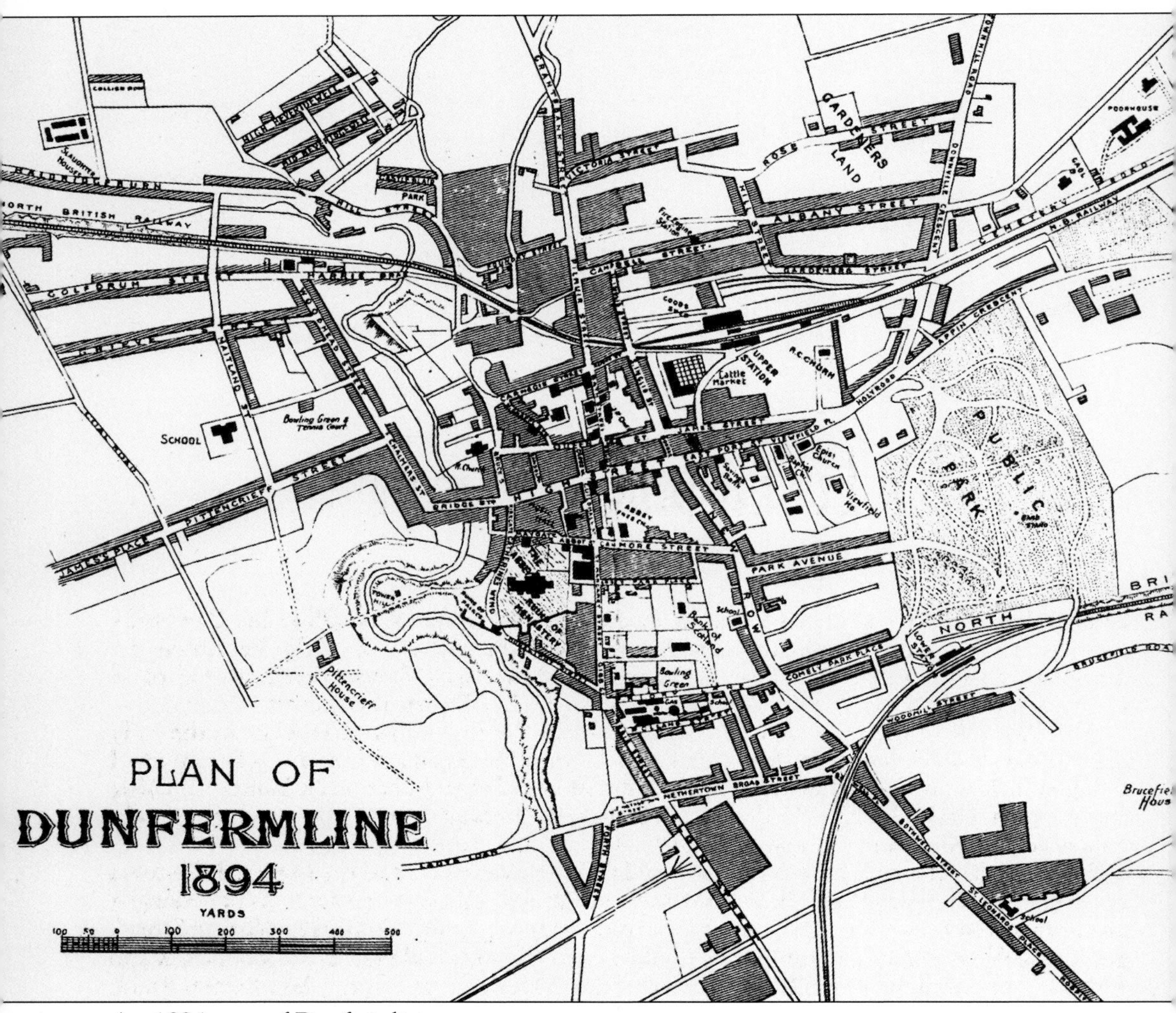

An 1894 map of Dunfermline.

Introduction

Dunfermline's history stretches back to medieval times when King Malcolm Canmore's marriage to the saintly Saxon princess, Margaret, set the seal on the town becoming the birthplace of several Scottish kings and princes. Malcolm and Margaret are both buried at Dunfermline Abbey, along with other royal Scots, including Robert the Bruce.

Although one of the royal capitals of Scotland, life for the ordinary townsfolk in the early days appears to have been a fairly humdrum affair, with the population of only a few hundred living in little more than a huddle of wooden shacks outside the Abbey walls. However, during the reign of David I (1124-1153) Dunfermline was granted 'burgh' status, which greatly enhanced its trading and economic prospects.

By the fifteenth century the population had risen to over 1,000 and the centre of the town as we know it, appears to have been fairly well established. The street pattern has not changed much since that time – Hiegate (High Street) ran east to west, with Collier Row (Bruce Street) and Cross Wynd extending northwards from it. From the south side ran St Catherine's Wynd with Maygate turning eastwards from it. New Row, Queen Anne Street (then Rotten Row), Priory Lane (then the Common Vennel) and Nethertown were also in place.

By the eighteenth century Dunfermline's cottage weaving industry was well established and, by the middle of the following century, several steam-powered linen weaving factories were coming on stream to ensure the town's credentials as a major player in this industry. This, together with the development of coal mining, the opening of the naval dockyard at Rosyth, and the introduction of other industries, has seen the population of the town rise to its present day figure of well over 50,000.

The intention of this book is to provide a photographic look at the development of road transport in the town over the past century and to highlight some of the changes that have been necessary, and perhaps some that were not so necessary, to accommodate the motor car. In addition it is hoped that sufficient information has been included on many of Dunfermline's buildings and businesses to whet the appetite of those who might not solely be interested in what makes the wheels go round.

The dawn of the twentieth century, of course, more or less coincided with the arrival of the motor car in this country and, like most aspects of life over the past 100 years, the development of road transport has progressed at a pace our forebears could not have anticipated. Horse-drawn carts and carriages, over unmade roads and country tracks, with journey times being measured in days rather than hours, was still the order of the day when the new century dawned. As we now enter the twenty-first century the country is scarred in all directions with two, three and four lane motorways, along which motor cars, buses and even 40 ton lorries can travel in a fraction of that time.

Quite what Dunfermline's royal forefathers would have made of the town as it is today is anyone's guess. What, for example, would Malcolm's thoughts be about the decision to infill the Tower Burn ravine, containing the cave where his beloved Margaret sought solitude, to create something as basic as a car park. On a lighter note, what would they have made of the 'magic roundabout' at Sinclair Gardens, and would they have understood the concept of the pedestrian scheme in the High Street area that appears to lean more favourably towards motorists than to those on foot?

In compiling this book I am indebted to the following who provided information and, where applicable, for allowing photographs to the re-produced:

Chris Neale and the staff of the Local History Department of Dunfermline Carnegie Library, Dunfermline Press Group, Edith May, Kate and Fiona Goodall, Tom Gibson, Ronnie Morris, Ian Whitehead, Margaret Cassidy (nee Jackson), Jimmy Allison, Anne Harris, John Johnston, Blyth MacFarlane, Tom Penny, Bill Spence, Arlene Best, Douglas Scott, Gordon Hill, David Sinclair, Matthew Cousin, Innes Cameron, Jack Rennie and Aerofilms Limited. Thanks also to Carnegie Dunfermline Trust from whose Twentieth Century Dunfermline Project this book has evolved. Finally, my thanks to my wife, Liz for her forbearance during the many hours I was absent from normal duties, and for providing the odd cup of coffee during the times she was still speaking to me.

George Beattie, November 2001.

One
Street Scenes

Photographs of street scenes probably reflect better than anything else how a town changes over the years and Dunfermline is no exception as this section will show. From cobbled streets in the central area of the town to country lanes on the outskirts, we see progress over the years with road widening schemes, better road surfaces, improved street lighting and any amount of traffic lights, keep left signs and double yellow lines. These scenes will hopefully also reflect the commercial changes, particularly in the town centre which, in the early and middle parts of the century, was highly regarded as an area to visit, not only for its places of historical interest, but as an excellent shopping area. The trend towards out of town supermarkets and a lack of forward planning has reduced the High Street area to a shadow of its former vibrant self. On the positive side it has to be said that during the early years of the century Dunfermline was fortunate to have its famous son, Andrew Carnegie, who provided the finance for many of the splendid buildings existing in the town today. Above we see the great man in 1902, with his wife Louise, probably in one of John Goodall's fine horse-drawn carriages, making their way from High Street into Bonnar Street, en route to Pilmuir Street, where Mrs Carnegie would lay the memorial stone for the new Carnegie Baths and Gymnasium. In the background James Dick, the grocer (later to be D.C.I.), is promoting Vanguard Old Scotch Whisky.

We start our look at Dunfermline's street scenes with this *c.*1875 view of the Kirkgate with the spire of the 'auld toon hoose' (demolished in 1876) in the background. The Abbey Tavern and the Old Inn hostelries on the left are still in place to this day. The dapper gent at the door of the Abbey Tavern might well be the landlord, James Cowan, in whose family the business remained until the 1960s.

The new Town House, at the corner of Kirkgate and Bridge Street, starts to take shape. It was completed in 1879, for the princely sum of £20,000, and today, more than 120 years later, the skills of the craftsmen of that era are still plain for all to see. The stonemasons engaged on the building work would manhandle most of the large stone blocks featured in this scene into position.

Looking west towards the then recently completed Town House from the Cross, this *c.*1885 High Street scene shows two horse-drawn delivery carts along with a significant number of men, including a police officer, all of whom are taking a keen interest in the photographer. Note the ornamental gas street lamp, which featured at the Cross for many years.

The year is now 1898 and John Jamieson's gents clothing shop, featured in the previous photograph on the corner of High Street and Cross Wynd, has been demolished to make way for a new building, under construction for the North of Scotland Bank (now occupied by the Clydesdale Bank). Further west on High Street the scene is busy with horse-drawn carts and carriages.

Wheelbarrows and handcarts are the order of the day at the lower end of High Street whilst further up the street a pony and trap makes its way towards The Cross. Lipton the grocer's shop is on the immediate left with Tyler's boot and shoe shop on the right. The impressive building at the middle left is the new Dunfermline Co-operative Society Department Store, which opened in 1901.

The Cross is the location in this *c.*1905 scene as a lone horse-drawn coach makes its way up High Street on a sunny afternoon. In this postcard the artist's pencil has been put to good use to bring the Town House more sharply into focus, a trick of the trade often used in the early days of photography. For some reason the pedestrian traffic on the High Street is again male dominated, apart that is, from the elegant young lady on the left.

Looking from the High Street into Bridge Street this early Edwardian scene shows to good effect the combination of French and Gothic styles of architecture used in the building of the Town House. The clock spire was added as an afterthought and was designed so that the 'toon clock' could be read from any location in the town.

Virtually the same scene as above, a decade or so further on, and we now see that the far end of Bridge Street has been opened up to give public access to Pittencrieff Park. The park was purchased in 1902 by Andrew Carnegie for £45,000 and gifted to the people of Dunfermline the following year. Among the trees in the distance is Carnegie's statue, erected in 1914, and paid for by public subscription in recognition of 'his many princely gifts to his native city'.

Fairfield Stores advert.

THE DUNFERMLINE DIRECTORY.

NICOL,

The Famed Hatter,

Hosier, & Outfitter

HAS always the **Largest, Choicest, & Best Selected Stock** in the Kingdom of Fife.

SILK and FELT HATS CAPS, TIES, GLOVES, CUFFS, COLLARS, and FRONTS (The Latest London Novelties)

The Best Productions in WHITE SHIRTS, REGATTA SHIRTS, TENNIS, GOLFING, & CYCLING SHIRTS.

READY-MADE CLOTHING of Every Description

BOYS' and YOUTHS' SUITS A Speciality.

WATER-PROOF COATS, TRAVELLING BAGS, UMBRELLAS, HOSIERY.

2 High Street and 2 Bruce Street, Dunfermline

27

Nicol advert.

1899 and the crowds turn out to welcome the Earl of Elgin back to the town from a five year engagement as Viceroy and Governor-General of India. Note the hussars on horseback with swords drawn and the soldiers with fixed bayonets controlling the throngs on Kirkgate. The shop in the background is that of Robert Nicol, the hatter, who would later move further up the High Street to the Cross Wynd junction.

An early Gala Day parade with the schoolchildren of Dunfermline making their way down the High Street en route from the Public Park to Pittencrieff Park where a day of fun and games would ensue. The Gala was another of Andrew Carnegie's gifts, designed to bring 'sweetness and light into the monotonous lives of the toiling masses of the town'. Note the Commercial Temperance Hotel on the right.

Now around 1915 and this busy summer scene on the High Street indicates that, whilst the horse is still the primary mode of transport, things are changing with a tramcar and an early motor car both making their way towards the Town House. The Dunfermline Press Office is at the corner of Guildhall Street whilst Saunder's Tearoom on the High Street appears to be getting a delivery of milk from the cart parked outside. Note the youngsters apparently quite happy to run about the street barefoot.

Moving eastwards along High Street now and looking towards East Port, this *c.*1920 scene shows a pony and trap, with uniformed driver, straddling the tramlines. The handcarts on the right could well be making a delivery of laundry to Inglis' Royal Hotel, a prominent establishment in the town until the 1970s when much of the south side of the street was re-developed.

Still around 1920 and an open-top tramcar, probably bound for Lochore, makes its way along High Street towards the New Row junction. The building on the immediate right housed a branch of Dick's Co-operative Institution (D.C.I.) and the bill board outside states that therein you could partake of a three course lunch for one shilling (5p) or a 'Dainty Tea' for fourpence (approx. 2p). Changed days indeed!

The motor car is beginning to make its presence felt on the High Street, *c.*1925, although there is still plenty of room on the roadway for the menfolk of the town to congregate whilst they put the wrongs of the world to right. The sign below the top window on the gable end of the Press Office proclaims, 'Alcoholic Drinks Must Be Voted Out'.

Early 1930s and the motor car has well and truly arrived on the High Street with a bull-nose Morris Tourer nearest to the camera. Woolworth's 3d and 6d Store opened on the south side of the street in 1922 before moving to larger premises across the road in 1938. In the distance it appears that the new Glen Gates are in place.

A Tilling-Stevens bus makes its way up High Street at the end of a journey from Stirling. At this time, prior to the opening of the Glen Bridge, all east/west traffic through Dunfermline had to make its way via the High Street. This particular photograph was taken from the top deck of a tramcar and shows that Hepworths, the gent's outfitter, have now moved into the former Dunfermline Press premises. Nicol, the hatter, occupied the shop shown on the immediate right for many years.

Still around 1930, but further east along High Street, we see the sign for Maloco's Empire Billiard Casino, a favourite meeting place for the would-be Stephen Hendrys of the day. The two-storey building on the immediate left houses a fruit shop, aptly named Covent Garden, and a sign in its window says 'Eat more fruit – keep away flu'. This building would shortly be demolished to make way for the frontage of the new Regal Cinema.

Two significant changes to the High Street, *c.*1938, from the previous photograph – the tramlines have been lifted and the Regal Cinema, opened on 31 December 1931, is now in place. To the left of the Regal the sign for the Buttercup Dairy can just be seen and across the road is R.S. McColl's sweet shop. The imposing British Linen Bank building next door to R.S. McColl still exists but is now a McDonalds' fast food outlet.

A royal visit to Dunfermline during the summer of 1948, by King George VI, Queen Elizabeth and Princess Margaret, and here the royal cavalcade of cars make their way up the High Street, past the waving crowds, from the civic reception at the Music Pavilion in Pittencrieff Park.

This is Kirkgate, in the 1940s, with Dunfermline Abbey in the background. The Police Station sign can be seen on the ground floor of the Town House to the right. Although the main Police Station moved to Abbey Park Place in 1946, the cells at the Kirkgate were in use until 1972 when the new station opened at Holyrood Place. The tower of Blelloch's building can be seen on the left whilst the premises on the south side of Maygate was occupied by Fraser & Carmichael, the wholesale grocers.

A busy scene at the lower end of the High Street in the late 1940s and the reader can be excused for assuming that one-way traffic had been introduced as a Rumblingwell bound double decker makes its way past a line of pre-war motor cars. Not so, but it emphasises how congested the High Street had become by that time with two-way traffic. Tyler's boot and shoe shop is still in the same place almost fifty years on from when we first saw it (see page 12).

A one-way traffic system (eastbound) was introduced to the High Street in 1951, as can be seen from this middle 1950s view. Graftons, the ladies' outfitters, occupy the former D.C.I. building on the right, whilst that on the left is occupied by D.I. Hunter, the grocers. A Hillman Minx car of the day can be seen approaching the New Row where the policeman on points duty could well be Constable John Penman, who for many years controlled traffic at this junction in his own inimitable fashion.

High noon on the High Street, probably around 1939, as a Townhill bound bus trundles past the new Woolworth's Store on the north side of the street. Smith, the pork butcher's shop is next door with Kilpatrick, the hairdresser, above. On the south side of the street the shops include Hepworth's, the gents outfitters; Bruce, the baker (with the Bruce Café above); Boots, the chemist; and the Buttercup Dairy. The all-male debating society is still meeting at the Cross.

Mid-afternoon, thirty years on from the top photograph, and some subtle changes have taken place on the High Street. The Rumblingwell / Townhill bus route is still via the High Street but Woolworths has had a facelift; Kilpatrick has moved with the times and is now Jacques, the hair stylist; whilst the Clydesdale Bank has replaced the North of Scotland Bank. Further down the street the tall building is part of the new Co-op complex in Randolph Street. Also, the ladies are at last taking to the street.

A last look at the High Street at the end of the century and all is not well. The street has been pedestrianised, or as the local authority quaintly entitled it 'a pedestrian favoured zone'. This description is something of a misnomer as numerous vehicles are still allowed to traverse through the street, regularly endangering the well-being of the pedestrians. Another sad indication of the times is the boarded-up and derelict Co-op premises, on the left, which have lain in this state for about twelve years.

WHY WALK WHEN YOU CAN RIDE IN LUXURY?

RING UP 447.

Cars to be had at Stance, Maygate, opposite Library, from 10 a.m. till 11 p.m., Sundays included.

Closed and Open Motors for Hire at Reasonable

Terms by Day, Week, or Month.

Phone No. 447.

J. BEATTIE, *MOTOR HIRER,*

28 Guildhall Street. DUNFERMLINE.

J. Beattie advert.

THE DUNFERMLINE DIRECTORY.

S. HODGSON,

Wholesale & Retail China & Waste Merchant,

ST CATHRINE'S WYND (Foot of Kirkgate),

DUNFERMLINE.

ALWAYS on Stock a Large Assortment of CHRYSTAL and CHINA to suit all Families. GLASS of every description supplied to Hotels and Restaurants at Lowest Prices.

Inspection Invited, and a Trial Solicited.

THOMAS DONALD, Junr.,

Tailor & Clothier,

38 CHALMERS STREET,

DUNFERMLINE.

18

Hodgson advert.

We move now into East Port, *c.*1920, looking towards the High Street/New Row junction from where a Lochore bound tramcar leaves the tramline loop. Prominent on the north side of East Port is the long established Ross's umbrella and leathergoods shop (see the raised umbrellas over the shop canopy). An early open-top motor car appears about to turn left and make the precarious descent of the New Row.

School's out in this middle 1940s shot of East Port outside Commercial Primary School with probably one of the first 'lollipop' men in the town stopping traffic to allow the children across the road. On the left can be seen the canopy of the Cinema Picture House whilst just beyond it is the sign for Kay Bruce's sweet shop, visited by cinema patrons for many years. Trundling eastwards is an S&D (Shelvoke & Drury) council refuse lorry, still running on solid tyres.

During the 1920s much road widening was carried out in Dunfermline, not only to improve matters for the increasing numbers of motor vehicles but also to provide employment in the area as a result of Rosyth Dockyard being run down following the first world war. The above photograph shows the East Port/James Street junction prior to the demolition of the corner shop building which allowed for the widening of East Port as seen below.

Now into Bridge Street shortly after the turn of the century and the horse-drawn bus outside The City Arms Hotel is probably that of Tom Cousin from Culross, who ran a service between Culross and Dunfermline. The City Arms (now The City Hotel) was an old posting inn and the archway to the left led to the hotel stables. The under-noted advertisement from 1898 outlines the various fine facilities the hotel was then able to offer potential customers.

CITY ARMS HOTEL,

Bridge Street, Dunfermline.

VISITORS To DUNFERMLINE will find the above HOTEL the Largest, most Comfortable and Central in Town. The Hotel contains Large COMMERCIAL ROOM, PUBLIC & LADIES COFFEE ROOMS, PRIVATE SUITES OF APARTMENTS, Spacious STOCK-ROOMS, DINING HALL for Large Parties, BILLIARD ROOM; HOT, COLD, and SHOWER BATHS

Visitors should particularly note that this is the ONLY HOTEL in Town that can Supply the above-mentioned Accommodation.

OMNIBUSES ATTEND ALL TRAINS AND CONVEY PASSENGERS TO AND FROM THE HOTEL.

Suitable Guide always in readiness to conduct Visitors to the Abbey, &c.

LAURENCE ANDERSON, Proprietor.

A tramcar edges into Bridge Street from Chalmers Street in this scene from around 1915. Bridge Street was home to a number of quality shops at this time such as the Fairfield Drapery Stores and David Hutton, the ladies outfitter, on the left. On the immediate right is the bookshop of James McPherson, who would later move his business to the Regal Close and subsequently to Chalmers Street. Another long-time inhabitant of Bridge Street was the pharmaceutical chemist, David Gilmour whose turn of the century advertisement (below) clearly indicates that the chemists of the day were skilled in much more than just dispensing cough remedies.

DAVID GILMOUR,

Pharmaceutical Chemist & Seedsman,

40 BRIDGE STREET, DUNFERMLINE.

A Large and Select Stock of PHARMACEUTICAL, AGRICULTURAL, VETERINARY, & PHOTOGRAPHIC DRUGS and CHEMICALS.

Edinburgh, or Local, ÆRATED WATERS in Syphons or Small Bottles.

HAIR BRUSHES, NAIL BRUSHES, TOOTH BRUSHES, SHAVING BRUSHES, DRESSING COMBS, SPONGES, FLESH GLOVES, and other Toilet Requisites in great Variety.

Choice Selection of TOILET SOAPS, PERFUMERY, &c.

Patent and Proprietary MEDICINES, as introduced.

ELASTIC GOODS, STOCKINGS, BANDAGES, HOT WATER BOTTLES, TRUSSES, &c.

Wholesale and Retail KITCHEN GARDEN and FLOWER SEEDS, DUTCH AUTUMN BULBS, etc., etc.

Careful Attention to Supplying only SEEDS of TESTED GERMINATING PROPERTIES, at strictly Moderate Prices.

Stock Large and Fresh in their Seasons.

Special Mixture of LAWN GRASS SEEDS for Tennis Courts, Bowling and Golf Greens, Lawns, etc., etc.

CLUBS SUPPLIED ON SPECIAL TERMS.

BIRD SEEDS of every Kind; also, Capern's Specialties, Sundries, etc., etc.

Bridge Street in the early 1920s looking towards the original wooden Glen Gates with Andrew Carnegie's statue in the background. The two-storey building on the left, housing McPherson's bookshop and the ironmongery shop of Coull and Matthew, would shortly be demolished to make way for the Louise Carnegie (wife of Andrew) Gates (seen below), which were completed in 1929 and provided an impressive entrance to Pittencrieff Park. The stable entrance to the immediate right in the photograph below still exists on Bridge Street, although it no longer echoes to the sound of horses' hoofs.

Round the corner now into Chalmers Street and the above photograph from the turn of the century shows the Bridge Street / Chalmers Street corner before the Glen Gates arrived. Hand-barrows feature as the transport of the day although there is also evidence of a horse having recently passed that way. The photograph below, from around 1930, illustrates the number of Chalmers Street shops that had to go to make way for the Glen Gates.

Horse-drawn carriages and tramcars compete for space on Chalmers Street in this Edwardian scene. William Ferguson's florist shop (on the right) existed on Chalmers Street until the late 1960s – see advert right. The church further up the street, which was variously a church, a masonic lodge and a furniture warehouse, was demolished in the 1960s to provide an access to Chalmers Sreet Car Park – see pages 36 and 37.

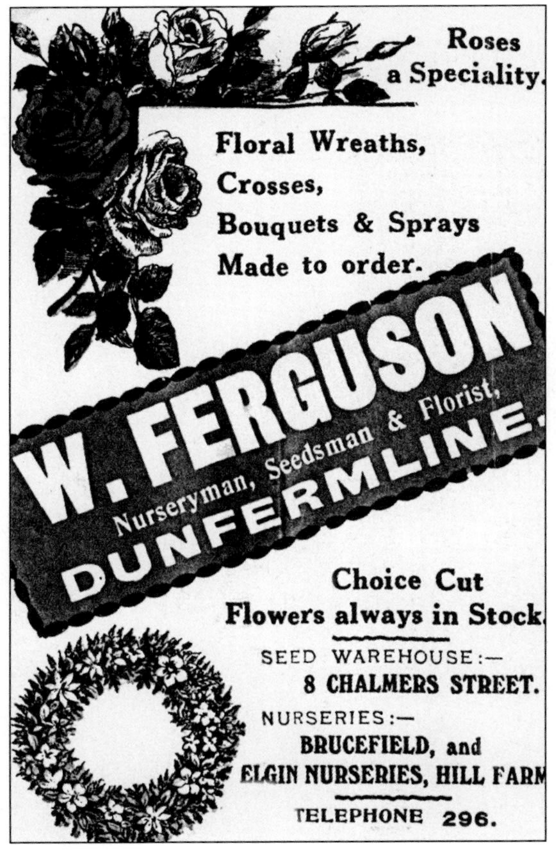

This is Pittencrieff Street at its junction with Chalmers Street, probably in 1930, just prior to the buildings containing the shop premises of Adam Masterton, House Furnisher, in Chalmers Street being demolished to make way for the building of the Glen Bridge. The Crown Tavern, to the left on Pittencrieff Street, remained a watering hole for the locals until suffering a similar fate in early 1970s.

Across the Tower Burn ravine now and into Carnegie Street (now Carnegie Drive), at its junction with Bruce Street, and the buildings facing the camera on Bruce Street also await demolition in anticipation of the new Glen Bridge. The building on the left was the town's Model Lodging House – see Page 40. The partly demolished building on the right is part of the old Caledonia Linen Works, destroyed by fire in 1925.

Opened on 20 April, 1932, by Provost Thomas Gorrie, the Glen Bridge formed a much need link between Pittencrieff Street and Carnegie Street and, in present day terms, it still forms an integral part of the main east/west route through the town. Spanning an 80ft deep ravine, the bridge was built in seventeen months by Townhill building contractors, Thomas Street & Co., at a cost of £40,379. Apart from some remedial work in the 1980s the bridge has stood the test of time well. The photograph below appears to indicate that the men-folk of the town have found a new meeting place.

Following the opening of the Glen Bridge most buses arriving in the town from the east and west soon found a temporary bus stance just off Carnegie Street on the site of the former Caledonia Linen Works – see page 95. The above photograph shows two early Alexander's buses travelling over the bridge towards the new stance and another heading out of the town probably destined for Glasgow or Stirling. Although tramcars continued to operate in Dunfermline until 1937, their demise was obviously in sight as the Glen Bridge was never thought of as a tram route.

MELDRUM & DAWSON

MOTOR COACH HIRERS

PRIVATE TOURS ARRANGED

WE AIM TO SATISFY

TERMS ON APPLICATION

WE CATER FOR YOUR
COMFORT AND PLEASURE

101 ST MARGARET'S STREET

DUNFERMLINE

Telephone: DUNFERMLINE 1681

Meldrum & Dawson advert.

Now into the 1960s and a decision was taken by the local authority which caused outrage in many quarters of Dunfermline. This was the project to fill in the Tower Burn ravine in the area bounded by Chalmers Street, Glen Bridge, Bruce Street and Bridge Street, for use as a car park. The cause of concern was that this area contained St Margaret's Cave, with its historical interest originating in the eleventh century. Undaunted, the powers that be went ahead and in the photograph below we see the construction of the tunnel that would lead from ground level to allow visitors access to the cave.

In the above scene the car park is almost at finished level and the shopkeepers and householders in the area were then complaining about the noise and dust nuisance. Most of the in-fill came from an old pit bing at Wellwood. The lower photograph shows the completed car park with its entrance from Chalmers Street and, in the foreground, the stairway leading to the contentious cave. The entrance to the stairway has since been reconstructed to provide a proper reception area for visitors to the cave.

Following page: This aerial photo of central Dunfermline from around 1955 reflects many of the changes to this area since that period: 1) Willie MacFarlane's yard – now a housing development; 2) The Tower Burn ravine – now a car park; 3) Winterthur's Silk Mills – now a furniture warehouse; 4) Hay & Robertson's Linen Works – now a housing development; 5) Dunlop Textiles – still there; 6) The top bus station – now the Fire Station car park; 7) Kinema Picture House – now a car park; 8 & 9) Goodall's Garage and the Union Inn – now Kingsgate Arcade;

1
2
10
14

4
3
5
6
7
8
9
12
13
11

Continued from p.37: 10) St Margaret's Hall – now part of the Carnegie Library. 11) St. Paul's Church – now a car park; 12) Joe Maloco's Billiard Hall – snookered! 13) Regal Picture House – now Littlewoods Store; 14) The bottom bus station – now a car park; 15) Dunfermline Police Station – now a social work office; 16) Alhambra Picture House – now a bingo hall. St Margaret's Hall was destroyed by fire in 1961, whilst St Paul's Church, Maloco's Billiard Hall and the Regal Picture House all suffered the same fate when the latter caught fire in 1976.

Into Bruce Street (North) now (or Damside Street as it was known until 1934) and we see what is probably the demolition of the buildings on the right to make way for the Glen Bridge. The large building in the background was opened in 1900 as a model lodging house and could accommodate 200 men and women. Segregation was then in force as the women's entrance was in Chapel Street whilst the men entered from Bruce Street. The lower photograph has been taken from the top floor of the lodging house looking into Damside Street, also in the early 1930s. Canmore Works, on the right, was opened in 1867 by J & T Alexander, Linen Manufacturers, and from 1932 until 1970 was occupied by Winterthur Silks, a Swiss based company. The fields in the background, of East Baldridge Farm, are now engulfed in housing.

Still in the early 1930s and round the corner from Damside Street into Mill Street we see how narrow this street was until 1934 when it was widened and a new retaining wall was built to hold back the gardens of the houses in Castleblair Park. The houses in the distance would be adjacent to Harriebrae Mill. The photograph below, taken in 1998, shows the widened street and the retaining wall but not much else has changed over the intervening sixty odd years.

The cobbled setts of old Baldridgeburn.

Looking east along Baldridgeburn from William Street prior to road widening in the 1920s we see what appear to be small gardens in front of the houses on the north side of the road. These were lost when Baldridgeburn was widened and the resulting railings, etc (see below) must have made it difficult for the coalman, on the left, to make his deliveries. A different era as well when the lady in the foreground would bring her own seat along to have a chat with her neighbour. Nearly all the houses in both photographs were demolished in the 1950s and 1960s.

In this 1930s scene, at the north end of William Street at its junction with Rumblingwell, we see, on the left beside the early telephone box, James Hunter, the general merchant's shop and on the right the Co-op butchery shop. The railway bridge carried the Dunfermline / Stirling railway line whilst the factory chimney in the background would be that of Gilbert Rae's Baldridge Lemonade Works.

From the same era but now looking north on William Street from its junction with Golfdrum Street we see the tramlines which extended out to Parkneuk. The entrance on the left gave access to the Colton railway sidings where Peter Y. Garden operated a paraffin oil depot for many years. The chimney-stack in the distance above the railway bridge would be that of Blackburn Iron Foundry, owned by the McLeod family.

Still in the 1930s and now at the east-end of Goldrum Street where we see a gent looking down Chalmers Street from a leisurely position under an old gas lamp. The advertising hoarding promotes the delicacies of the day such as Camp Coffee, Nestles Milk, Farola Biscuits, Oxo Cubes and even the Murphy Radio. The changes to Golfdrum Street over the years can be seen in the lower photograph although the cobbled roadway leading into Buffies Brae still exists.

Down to St Margaret's Street now, at its junction with Monastery Street, and the former Abbey Gardens steam-powered linen works of Henry Reid & Son, which operated from 1860 to 1928, is being demolished. This site would later become St Margaret's Bus Station or, as it was more commonly known, the 'bottom bus stance', servicing the areas to the south of the town.

Into the 1950s and further up St Margaret's Street we see, on the left, St Margaret's Halls where many Dunfermline couples spent Saturday nights dancing to Jim Brown's band. Sadly, the halls were burnt to the ground in 1961 in one of the town's worst fires of the century. On the opposite side of the street are the garage premises of the Fife Motor Company (now a night club) and beyond that St Margaret's Hotel, at that time a favourite with the sailors of Rosyth Dockyard.

Back in time now to the turn of the century and we are at the top of the New Row at its junction with East Port. Most of the buildings in this scene were demolished around 1910 to make way for the new Bank of Scotland building which opened in 1912. Was this photograph perhaps taken by J.K. Munro, the photographer and portrait painter who had the studio on the corner of East Port and whose advertisement from 1895 can be seen below?

J. K. MUNRO,

Dunfermline Photographic Studio,

1 East Port Street.

(Top of New Row),

DUNFERMLINE.

OUTSIDE GROUPS SPECIALLY ATTENDED TO.

Down the New Row now to its junction with Comely Park Place and we can see how narrow this street became as it descended towards the railway viaduct. This problem had been exacerbated by the introduction in 1918 of the tram route to Rosyth Dockyard. However, in 1924 this part of the New Row was substantially widened as can be seen below and this remained the main route into the town from the south until 1986, when St Margaret's Drive opened and the bottom end of New Row was closed to traffic.

Around 1937 and this is New Row, at its junction with Canmore Street, with an Austin 10 motor car of that era making its way down the steep descent from the High Street. Fraser's grocery shop is on the corner of Canmore Street and this, along with all other buildings northwards on that side of New Row would be demolished in the 1970s to make way for Littlewoods complex.

The bottom of the New Row (on the right), with Bothwell Place to the left, in the late 1950s. Not surprisingly, this junction was known locally as 'the gusset'. The building in the foreground containing a branch of the Co-op Bakery, was demolished around 1970 as part of a road improvement scheme. The viaduct in the background carries the Dunfermline/Edinburgh railway line and was built in 1877.

Bothwell Street in the early 1920s with the wrought iron fencing on the right fronting the prestigious linen factory premises of Erskine Beveridge. Shortly after this photograph was taken the parapet of the Spittal Bridge (in the foreground) was moved further to the left as part of road widening project, with the existing stone pillars being re-used. These and the houses beyond have since gone and the roadway is now a dual-carriageway.

With the central area of Dunfermline as a backdrop, a horse-drawn cart (complete with rear gunner) and an Alexander's bus make their way down Hospital Hill, probably in the middle 1930s. The Tollgate Garage can be seen further down the street and a sign of the times are the massive telegraph poles lining the east side of the street.

Back up the town now to Pilmuir Street. It is around 1902 and above we see the cottages on the right being demolished to make way for the new Carnegie Baths and Gymnasium seen below. This was one of the many public buildings gifted to the town around that time by Andrew Carnegie. The building on the left was the Pilmuir Linen Works of Andrew Reid Ltd which, in 1926, was acquired by Hay & Robertson Ltd and subsequently passed to the Dunlop Rubber Company in 1947 for use as a textile spinning mill.

Round the corner now into Foundry Street in the early 1930s with (above) Hay & Robertson's Linen Works on both sides of the street. The 'bridge of sighs' between the buildings was erected around 1929, after the Pilmuir Works was acquired, and was designed to aid the passage of workers between the two buildings. The photograph below shows the opposite end of Foundry Street, still with Hay & Robertson works on both sides of the road. Only three gas lamps can be seen throughout the length of the street and in the winter months this must have been a rather bleak area for the hundreds of mill girls going to and from work.

Still the early 1930s and this is Reform Street, probably on a Saturday evening with (above) an orderly queue waiting for the 'second house' at the Opera House, whilst below we see the 'first house' coming out. It was a sign of the times that people queued on the roadway leaving the pavement clear for others making their way to their homes. Opened in 1903, the Opera House was the town's premier theatre for many years until its closure in 1955 and regularly played host to music hall legends such as Sir Harry Lauder, Will Fyffe and 'the voice of Scotland', Robert Wilson.

A street from yesteryear – this is Queen Anne Street in the middle 1960s looking west from Bonnar Street. A decade or so later the buildings on both sides of this street would disappear to make way for the Kingsgate Centre. For the record the premises on the north side were the Union Inn; R.C. Ferguson, the florist; Cooper, the grocer; then Goodall's Garage. On the immediate left was Grant's furniture shop.

Another street to undergo radical change in the late 1970s was James Street with the development of the new bus station and the multi-storey car park. Upper Station Road (to the left where the two men are walking) disappeared completely at that time. The building in the distance with the six pane windows was originally Robert Philp's Garage, later to be occupied by Bob Bernard, the taxi operator.

Known locally as the Park Gates junction, this is where Townhill Road and Appin Crescent met as seen above in the 1930s. The small house in the foreground is believed to have been a toll-bar under the old turnpike road system. In the lower scene from the 1950s the house, along with the tramlines, has gone and keep-left islands are now in place to regulate the ever-increasing traffic. The large building on the corner was the Park Tavern; with John Donald, the draper, next door.

Early spring, in the late 1950s and P.C.No. 2 Bob Wilson leads the St George's Day parade of Scouts and Guides into the Public Park from Holyrood Place. The cottages on the right were demolished around 1970 to make way for the development of Carnegie Drive and Sinclair Gardens Roundabout. The two-storey building at the far end of the cottages was formerly Bunckle's Holyrood Rope Works and was latterly occupied by Gray, the furniture removers.

This was the west carriageway of the Public Park, which ran from the Park Gates south to the Lower Railway Station and Comely Park. It was replaced in 1986 by the dual carriageway of St Margaret's Drive, but not before much controversy as the new road cut a massive swath through the park.

The creation of Sinclair Gardens Roundabout (above) in 1972 saw the removal of the Park Tavern and a number of other buildings at the old Park Gates junction. On the left (above) the town's new Police Station (opened in November, 1972) edges in view. Below, we see how the roundabout has become the hub for all main roads in the town and has inevitably become the locus of many accidents, and many more near misses. Not one of the road planners' better ideas!

The bottom of Townhill Road in the early 1930s and (above) we see what appears to be a motor cyclist making his way, between the tramlines, up the first of the three steep inclines towards Townhill. Many early motor cars, such as the one on view, had very poor brakes and it to be hoped that the children on the roadway managed to get onto the pavement before it got too close to them. Not much has changed in this scene over the intervening seventy years. In the scene below we make it to the thinner air at the top of Townhill Road where we see two open top tramcars plying the route between Townhill and Rumblingwell. You were pretty well off if you had a house in Townhill Road at that time.

From the north-east corner of the town to the south-west now and this is Forth Street, looking towards West Nethertown, in the early 1920s. Judging by the pails on the pavement it must be 'bucket day'. In the lower photograph, taken a few years later, and looking from West Nethertown towards Forth Street and Milton Green, we see that municipal housing has replaced the old cottages and that the road surface is much improved. The new houses would have electricity but gas lighting still prevails on the street. To the right is the original Nethertown entrance to Pittencrieff Park.

Above is Woodmill Road at its junction with Charles Street, probably in the 1940s. The gate on the right led to the grounds of Brucefield House. The scene below finds us a little further west on Woodmill Road with the entrance to Transylaw (now home to Commercial and St Margaret's Primary Schools) on the left. On the right are the fields of Brucefield Fues (now Rosebank Housing Estate, named after the rose fields belonging to William Ferguson). Woodmill Road was little more than a country lane at that time.

Following page: Highlighted in this 1932 aerial view of Dunfermline from the south-west are some landmarks of yesteryear: 1) Winterthur's Silk Mills (1932-1970); 2) Hugh Elder's Grain Mills (1908-approx. 1968); 3) St Paul's Church (1884-1976); 4) Regal Cinema (1931-1976);

1
3
6
10
11

2
5
8
9
13
14

Continued from p.59: 5) Alhambra Cinema (1922-?); 6) The former Abbey Garden Linen Works (1860-1928); 7) Dunfermline High School (1886-1939); 8) Lauder Technical School (1899-1970); 9) West Fife Hospital (1894-1993); 10) Nethertown Railway Sidings; 11) Ralph Stewart's Rubber Works (1900-1957); 12) Bothwell Linen Works (1865-1932); 13) Bothwell Linen Works Bleaching Pond; 14) Wilson & Wightman's Bruce Embroidery Works (?-1935).

We'll now take a trip out the 'east road', as the Appin Crescent/Halbeath Road area was known in the early days. This is Appin Crescent, at its junction with Garvock Hill, shortly after it was upgraded with dual tramlines in 1924. In the distance we see the Fife Motor Company (with an early petrol pump in the forecourt) and beyond that the turnstiles leading into East End Park.

Outside East End Park now about 1920 – yes, that's it on the right. Was the fence meant to keep people out or to keep the fans in? In the distance a horse-drawn coach can be seen passing the Fife Motor Company whilst a more modern form of transport sits outside one of the relatively new houses on Halbeath Road. The roadway was widened at this point in 1924.

Still at East End Park and, in 1961, the fans are queuing for tickets for Dunfermline's Scottish Cup Final clash with Celtic at Hampden Park where, after a replay, the 'Pars' returned to the town triumphant for the first time in their history. They would repeat this feat again in 1968, beating Heart of Midlothian 3-1.

It's now 1998 and Halbeath Road, outside East End Park, remains virtually the same although Dunfermline Athletic Football Club has progressed, at least in terms of ground improvements with a newly completed all-seated stadium. It's a long time since the team last won the Scottish Cup though.

Further out (east) Halbeath Road around 1920, and (above) we see, on the left, Dunfermline and West Fife Laundry. On the right is Garvock Farm, the steading of which was demolished in the 1960s to make way for Garvock Petrol Station. The farmhouse still exists, now in use as a guesthouse. In the scene below we see how the roadway was much improved in the mid 1920s.

The state of Halbeath Road appears to have worsened the further east you went from the town. Now (above) near Whitefield Road and it can be clearly seen how the roadway was lowered under the railway bridges to accommodate the double-decked tramcars introduced in 1909. Again (below) we can see how the road improvements of the 1920s transformed the area.

Above and below we see Halbeath Road at its junction with Whitefield Road in the early 1920s. The building on the right, by the parked car, (above) was Touch Bleachfield and on the left, further on, can be seen a steam road roller. In the lower photograph, taken from the opposite direction, a roadman's caravan can be seen parked at the entrance to Whitefield Road. Road improvements were about to start and would probably put a stop to the children gathering brambles at the roadside.

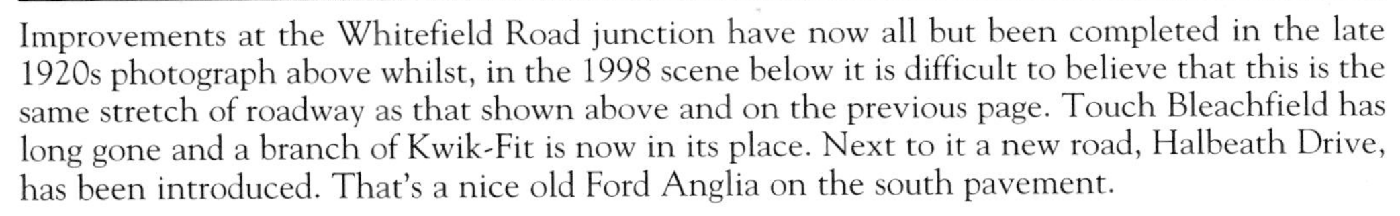

Improvements at the Whitefield Road junction have now all but been completed in the late 1920s photograph above whilst, in the 1998 scene below it is difficult to believe that this is the same stretch of roadway as that shown above and on the previous page. Touch Bleachfield has long gone and a branch of Kwik-Fit is now in its place. Next to it a new road, Halbeath Drive, has been introduced. That's a nice old Ford Anglia on the south pavement.

Whitefield Road wasn't left out of the road improvement schemes of the 1920s and, above, we see it in its original form. Was this the new meeting place for the menfolk of the town or is something interesting going on in the Lyne burn? Below, the road widening and resurfacing is ongoing with a solitary sign in the midst of it all saying 'Caution – Road Repairs', a little different from the cones of today. It is interesting to note the keep-left island being constructed at the junction – it may well have been the first in the town.

Two
Horse and Motor Transport

When the twentieth century dawned the railways were well established but on the roads it was still the trusty horse that provided the main means of transport, whether for the carriage of goods or the general public. Although the benefits of the motor vehicle were recognised early by some, many businesses retained horse transport until the 1940s. Indeed it was well into the 1970s before the last horse-drawn milk cart was withdrawn from service by Dunfermline Co-operative Society. The hilly terrain on which the town is built made sure the 'cuddies' plying its streets always put in a hard shift. The introduction of motor transport was not altogether trouble free and the town's narrow streets soon became a problem as traffic volume built up. In the 1920s much work was carried out to rectify this although many would suggest that even today Dunfermline is not an easy town to drive through. Around the turn of the century several horse-drawn bus operators worked the area around Dunfermline. All such businesses were licensed by the local authority and this one, owned by William Philp of St Margaret's Street, operated between Dunfermline and Saline. It was licensed to carry twelve passengers inside and four outside. The journey time to Saline took about one hour.

At the turn of the century the stabling facilities of John Goodall in Queen Anne Street were among the finest in the country (see also page 101). Above we see one of Goodall's brakes, with uniformed coachman, about to set off with a group from the Tormaukin Hotel at Glendevon. Are the passengers perhaps the local councillors on one of these fact finding trips? If so, it is to be hoped that none of these fine fellows fell off on the way back to Dunfermline. Below is another of Goodall's carriages with a goodly compliment of passengers, all in their Sunday best. There is no uniformed driver with this one – can it be an early instance of self-drive hire, and a lady driver at that.

In the era of the horse the steep New Row route into the town was an area to be avoided. Instead most used the Nethertown/Moodie Street/Monastery Street route, when coming from the south. Probably as a result of this Robert Reid ran a blacksmith's shop (the white building in the shadow of the Palace ruins above) in Monastery Street. Was this the first service-station in the town? Below we see Mr Reid (on the right with the beard) and his staff outside his premises. By the nature of their profession most blacksmiths were powerfully built men, but what about the stature of the constable next to him?

John Scott, the butcher, of 25 High Street, ran a number of horse-drawn vans during the period between the wars. Above, is butcher Jimmy Chalmers with an early van whilst, below, Sandy Arnott, who supplied the Valleyfield area, has a more modern van which has at least some weather protection for the driver. It is reputed that John Scott's horses excelled themselves at Hogmanay each year when the vanman might not have survived his customers' hospitality and the horse had to be relied upon to get them both home. Similarly, if a vanman was off work ill, another could take his place and could rely on the horse knowing the route and the houses at which to stop.

With clay pipe in his mouth, Sandy Watt, from Cairneyhill, was a familiar figure with his horse-drawn lorry, as he hawked ironmongery, chinaware, and waxcloth floor coverings around the villages to the west of Dunfermline. The location for this photograph is believed to be North Road, Saline.

William Stephen, the Baker, was another who relied on horse-drawn transport to get the bread and rolls to breakfast tables in the area. In this photograph it appears that the gaiter clad vanman, and his two lady customers, have all thrived on the plain white loaves displayed on the top shelf of his van.

Dick's Co-operative Institution (D.C.I.) almost rivalled the local Co-operative Society in the number of shops it had in the West Fife area during the early half of the century. A lover of horses, Mr Dick had excellent stabling facilities at his home at Transylaw and elsewhere in the town.

Built by George Dick, the Coachbuilder, Lochgelly, this type of horse-drawn bucket cart, capable of carrying $^3/_4$ of a cubic yard of refuse, was used by a number of local authorities. It is a little different from the 28 ton refuse collection vehicles of today. The sliding steel doors were, for some reason, known as Chelsea doors.

Dunfermline Co-operative Society made great use of horse-drawn vehicles in the early days and above we see butcher Tommy Chisholm on his round in the Brucefield area of the town, probably during the late 1920s. Tom went on to open his own butchery business in Townhill Road in 1946. He opened a further shop in Chalmers Street in the early 1960s, as well as operating travelling shops. The photograph below, taken in 1950, shows the Townhill Road shop with Tom on the right, the others being his father Tom, his brother Jim and shop assistant Martha Erskine. The Jowett Bradford motor van, bought new in 1948, cost £353.

Fruit and potato merchant, William (Wull) Best was another Dunfermline businessman who had a real passion for his horses. Above we see Wull, with his prized Clydedale, Ruth, going through her paces at an Agricultural Show. Ruth in fact won first place for Horse and Turn-Out, six times in a row, at the Royal Highland Show. For a Clydesdale Ruth's high-stepping technique was most unusual and more than one show judge questioned her pedigree. In the lower photograph Wull is keeping a watchful eye on grandson, Billy, in the saddle, whilst Ruth has come back down to earth as she resumes her day job of pulling the fruit cart round the streets of the town.

Time for the horse to have a snack as Gus Allan takes a break from serving penny sliders from one of Divito of Crossgates horse-drawn ice cream vans, probably at a children's gala somewhere in West Fife. Note how the reins pass through the lower middle window of the van, from where it would be driven.

William Keddie's horse-drawn chip vans were a familiar sight on the streets of Dunfermline until well into the 1950s. This van features a coal-fired fish-fryer and the device on the front ledge is a hand-operated potato chipper. The ornate design of this van was a feature of much of the horse transport of the era. These vans would travel as far afield as Links Market, in Kirkcaldy, and Burntisland Games.

The gent in the bowler hat, above, is David Williamson, who was a commercial traveller with Wm Cunningham & Co., Table Linen Merchants, of Chalmers Street. Mr Williamson travelled throughout the area by horse, visiting his customers and carrying his samples and orders in the wicker baskets seen on the cart. In the lower photograph Mr. Williamson has replaced the horse with a new (c.1920) Albion motor van. He has also discarded his heavy overcoat which was perhaps not a very wise move as the Albion looks to be at least as well air-conditioned as the cart.

Reputed to be the first petrol-powered horseless carriage in Dunfermline, this 6 $^{1}/_{2}$ horse-power, 1898 Daimler was owned by aerated water manufacturer, Gilbert Rae, of Baldridge Works, Golfdrum Street. Whilst built for the carriage of passengers, Mr Rae soon adapted the vehicle so that it could be used as a delivery vehicle during the week-days and for taking his family out into the country at week-ends. This vehicle remained at Baldridge Works until the factory closed in 1974, at which time it was bought and restored by the Scottish Transport Museum, Glasgow, where it is now on permanent display.

An interesting scene in Gilbert Rae's premises around 1912 when the company was in the process of changing over from horse to motor transport. Two of the lorries on the immediate left are early Commers, with solid tyres and chain driven rear wheels. In the early part of the century Rae had a depot in Falkirk that was serviced daily by horse-drawn lorry from Dunfermline – no mean feat when, prior to the opening of Kincardine Bridge in 1936, the route was via Stirling. In addition to lemonade, Gilbert Rae made ice blocks which were supplied to cold stores in shops, hotels, etc., in the days before freezers. In the lower photograph Rae's Granton motor lorry is part loaded with cases of lemonade and part with blocks of ice.

Driver Jim Paterson looks slightly apprehensive behind the wheel of David Brown's brand new Albion laundry delivery van, photographed outside the firm's Westfield Laundry works in Grieve Street. Ahead of its time, around 1914, with pneumatic tyres, the Albion was manufactured at Scotstoun, Glasgow, but the bodywork was built locally by George Kay & Sons, of Inglis Street.

Shortly after the First World War, Dunfermline Co-operative Society ran a fleet of the ubiquitous Model T Fords from their main premises at Randolph Street. Driver, Jimmy Fotheringham is seen here with one such vehicle, fitted with unusual solid tyres. These were perforated to give a cushioning effect but this was not a success and pneumatic tyres soon followed.

Tuesday was market day in Dunfermline and, for a few decades around the middle of the century, it was also the day for Stevenson's auction rooms. Based at 25 Bruce Street, William Stevenson ran a house furnishing and removal service in tandem with his popular auction rooms. Above we see Mr Stevenson and son, Ian, on the pavement, with van driver John Muir (at the van door) and others employees of the firm.

Like many other local authorities, the City and Royal Burgh of Dunfermline operated a fleet of S&D (Shelvoke and Drewry) refuse collection lorries, similar to the one above with driver, Harry Purves, and unknown colleague. These vehicles had a top speed of 19mph, a carrying capacity of only 1 ton, and were still operating on solid tyres until well after the Second World War.

The Buick van (above) was one of three such delivery vehicles operated by Dunfermline & West Fife Laundry, during the 1920s, from their Halbeath Road premises (the frontage of which is seen below around 1940). Run for over ninety years by three generations of the Hill family, the laundry had its origins in Moss-side Road, Cowdenbeath, where Mr & Mrs Charles Hill started the business in 1897.

During the early years of the Second World War, before they became actively involved, the USA rather covertly supplied assistance to the UK. One such scheme saw numerous US cities supply towns in the UK with tea wagons, such as the one above, which was presented to Dunfermline by the good citizens of Honolulu, Hawaii. The local dignitaries on parade are the Reverend Robert Dollar, Miss Staffiere, Lady Norval and James Moodie, Director of Music at the Music Institute, Bennachie, where these photographs were taken. Below we see the tea wagon in use with Lady Norval keeping a wary eye on the crockery.

Three
Trams and Buses

What arrived first in Dunfermline, the tramcars or the motor buses? Well, it appears to have been a close call as the first motor bus was licensed by Dunfermline Magistrates on 23 June 1909, whilst the first tramcar ran on 2 November, the same year. Trams were slow in making their appearance in Dunfermline when you consider that many towns had electric trams in service from around 1903, and some had horse-drawn trams long before that. However, when Dunfermline & District Tramway Company did get the go ahead from the authorities progress was swift. It took just over 100 men, working with pick and shovel, only ten weeks to install seven miles of tramlines, complete with overhead power supply, between East Port in Dunfermline and the High Street in Cowdenbeath (including a branch line from Dunfermline to Townhill). A tram depot was also constructed at Broad Street, Cowdenbeath. The only mechanical means used in the project was the use of steam navvies to lower the level of the roadway under the two railway bridges in Halbeath Road, in order to accommodate the proposed double decked tramcars. In this photograph we see the track-laying operations in East Port, during September, 1909. Tramcars operated in Dunfermline until 1937 when the power of the bus companies finally saw them off. It is perhaps ironic that tramcars are now making a reappearance in some areas of the country and are seen as a viable and modern form of public transport.

Tramcar No.1 passes the Park Gates on its way into Dunfermline from Cowdenbeath. This postcard is date-stamped 10 April 1910, and was sent to the author's grandmother, at Madderty, by her sister in Dunfermline, to show the new fangled machines that were conveying people about the streets of the town. Judging by the wintry scene it is likely that this photograph was taken on 2 November 1909, the day the trams were introduced to the town.

The weather is a bit better in this scene as Tramcar No.2 waits at the terminus in East Port, probably before setting off for Lochore. In the early years the tramline extended into the High Street, almost to the bottom of Douglas Street, but only to allow the trams to return to East Port, via the loop at the top of the New Row. The Bank of Scotland building on the corner of New Row was opened in 1912.

The Rumblingwell extension, via High Street, Bridge Street, Chalmers Street, Grieve Street and William Street, was opened on 27 December, 1913, with the terminus at the end of Parkneuk Road. In this Bridge Street scene, from around 1915, it can be seen how the tramlines splayed out at the corner of Chalmers Street in order to give each tram more room when passing at this tight turn.

With a single passenger on the top deck, Tramcar No.11 heads south on Chalmers Street, at its junction with Pittencrieff Street. In January, 1917, a tram service between Rumblingwell and Townhill, via the High Street, was introduced and so successful was it that a bus service was maintained on this route long after the trams had been withdrawn.

On 17 May 1918, a further extension from New Row to Rosyth Dockyard, via Bothwell Street, Hospital Hill, Queensferry Road, Kings Road, and Castle Road, was opened. This photograph shows a Dunfermline bound tram on the lines between the carriageways of Queensferry Road, this being the first dual carriageway in Scotland. There were, of course, no roundabouts on Queensferry Road at that time. When the trams ceased running, in 1937, the tram track on Queensferry Road became a cycle track.

The tram terminus at Rosyth Dockyard was on Hilton Road (above) but was nearly always referred to as the Dockgates terminus. The terminus at the Dunfermline end was on the New Row, at Canmore Street, as the final gradient up the New Row to High Street, was judged to be too steep for passenger safety. None-the-less this route was occasionally used for football specials.

In conjunction with the opening of the Rosyth Dockyard route, a new tram depot was opened at St Leonard's Street. St Leonard's depot then took over from the Cowdenbeath depot as the company's maintenance centre for the area. In this view, from the middle 1930s, the tram shed, with four lines entering, can be seen to the left with newer bus garages to the right.

Maintenance staff at St Leonard's tram depot line up for the photographer, probably around 1920. Can anyone name any of them? The La Scala Cinema, advertised on the stair treads of the left hand tram, was destroyed by fire on 13 April 1924, having occupied the old Music Hall premises in Guildhall Street from 2 October 1913.

The end of an era on 4 July 1937, as Dunfermline's tramcars finally give way to motor buses after some 28 years of faithful service. This photograph, at St Leonard's depot, shows one of the new fleet of double decked buses that replaced the tramcars overnight. Tramcar No.26 had been in service in the town from December 1912.

A sad sight in the late summer of 1937 as Dunfermline's recently retired tramcars are lined up on the reserved track between Crossgates and Hill of Beath. Many were scrapped there but a few were destined to survive in Fife for a number of years when they were converted to serve as holiday accommodation at a camping site in Kinghorn.

One of Dunfermline's earliest motor bus operators was Cousin's Motor Service, Culross, owned by brothers Tom and John Cousin, who ran services to many of the villages to west of the town from 1909 until 1925, when the company was acquired by the Scottish General Omnibus Co. of Falkirk. Above is Tom Cousin about to set off in his 1913 Commer, with what appears to be a fairly full compliment of passengers.

Like the Cousin brothers, William Philp, of St. Margaret's Street, originally ran horse-drawn buses in the town before moving on to motor buses in 1911. This photograph shows Mr Philp's second motor bus, also a Commer, acquired in 1913, with which he ran a service from Dunfermline to Limekilns and Charlestown. Note the size of the footbrake pedal – perhaps designed for both feet if one was not enough.

The village of Kelty had no fewer than four bus companies in the early 1920s, one of which was Kelty Motor Transport, founded in 1920 by William Milne and William McLean, with premises in Oakfield Street. They initially ran services between Dunfermline and Kelty, via the now lost village of Lassodie, but by 1929 were going as far afield as Cupar and St Andrews. This ex-First World War Maudsley, with 'state of the art' bus body, was the company's first vehicle.

Another Kelty bus operator of the 1920s was A.&A. Young (brothers Alex and Andrew) of Oakfield Terrace, who ran a service from Dunfermline to Kelty via Wellwood and Gask Toll. This Lancia was one of five such buses operated by the company between 1922 and 1931, when the firm was taken over by Alexander of Falkirk.

Dunfermline & District Tramways Company was always alive to the threat posed to the tramcars by the ever increasing number of motor bus operators in the area. In 1924, the company acquired about twenty motor buses, mainly Tilling-Stevens Petrol Electric vehicles of the type seen above, with the intention establishing itself as the main public transport operator in the area.

The opening of the Kincardine Bridge on 29 October 1936, made the Dunfermline area much more accessible to motorists from the west of Scotland, whilst reducing greatly the journey times from Dunfermline to Falkirk or Glasgow. This was the first bus to cross the bridge on opening day, an Alexander's Bluebird coach on the Dunfermline to Glasgow run.

During the Second World War the annual Childrens' Gala in the town was suspended. Using some of the funds normally used to run the gala, the Carnegie Dunfermline Trust commissioned the fitting out of this former bus as a mobile kitchen for use in the event of a war-time emergency in the area. Thankfully, the town and surrounding areas, including Rosyth Dockyard, escaped very lightly from the German bombers.

Touring buses were in great demand during the middle part of the century and several private firms were founded around Dunfermline to satisfy the demand for people to get out and about after the war years. One such firm was Rennie's Lion Coaches, founded by Jack Rennie of Cairneyhill in 1948, and which is still operating today. This scene shows Rennie's fleet lined up in Main Street, Cairneyhill, around 1960.

With the opening of the Glen Bridge in 1932, bus operators in the area soon found a suitable temporary bus stance (above) in Carnegie Street, on the site formerly occupied by the Caledonia Linen Works. A few years later this site became a permanent bus station, known locally as the 'top stance'. Below we see it around 1960, with the driver and conductress of the Ballingry bus posing for the photographer. The wooden building in the distance, adjacent to Jack Drummond's snack bar, was Alexander's booking office.

An early view of Alexander's booking office at the 'top stance' with the bill-boards outside giving details of the various evening and mystery tours on offer at that time. In addition to passenger transport, Alexander also provided a parcel service between the various towns visited by the buses and the young man in uniform in this scene probably delivered incoming parcels, on foot, around the town.

Where you have a 'top stance' it follows you must have a 'bottom stance' and Dunfermline's was in St Margaret's Street, servicing the Rosyth, Inverkeithing, Charlestown and coastal areas of Fife. Opened in the 1930s, on the site of the former Abbey Garden Linen Works, this bus station survived until the early 1970s. It was then incorporated into the 'top stance' for a few years, until the early 1980s, when the new bus station in Market Street was opened.

Market Street bus station was opened in 1984, partly on the site formerly occupied by the town's cattle market. Owned by Fife Council, with bus operators paying a stance fee each time they use the station. Above the bus station is a three-storey car park with its entrance in James Street being almost exactly where John Scott, the butcher, stabled his horses in the 1920s and 1930s.

Introduced by Stagecoach in 1996 on the Dunfermline to Glasgow route, this Volvo articulated seventy-one seater bus soon became known as the 'bendy bus'. In addition to the seventy-one seated passengers these buses are licensed to carry a further eight standing passengers but, rather ominously, they can only be in the front compartment. Nearly all buses are now one-man operated, with the days of the conductress shouting 'fares please' or 'come oan, get aff' having been consigned to history.

- - THE - -

Saline Motor Service,

109 MILL STREET,

- DUNFERMLINE. -

Daily Service between
DUNFERMLINE and SALINE.

Saturday & Sunday Service between
DUNFERMLINE & KINGSEAT, LASSODIE & KELTY

Popular Motor Tours in Highlands
:: during Summer Months. ::

PERSONAL SUPERVISION. REASONABLE TERMS.

Closed and Open Chars-a-banc
for Hire, for Private Parties,
Day or Night.

Proprietors:

J. H. CHISHOLM. J. BRAND, Junr.

TELEPHONE 37.

Saline Motor Service advert.

Travel by . . .

COMFORT COACHES

51 CARNEGIE STREET
DUNFERMLINE

★ Coaches and Double Decker Buses at your Disposal.

★ Social Outings, Picnics, Football fixtures, etc. specially catered for

★ 3 and 6-day Extended Tours.

★ MODERATE TERMS.

★ Modern Self-Drive Cars for Hire.

Telephones
Dunfermline
1275 & 2630

Comfort Coaches advert.

Travel in Luxury and Safety by . . .

SIMPSON'S Luxurious Motor Coaches

1 Market Street, DUNFERMLINE.

Simpson Coaches advert.

Telegrams: "GOODALL." Telephones. Works, No. 461. Hiring, No. 28.

JOHN GOODALL & CO.,

Motor Engineers and Agents,

58-60 Queen Anne St., DUNFERMLINE.

Sole Agents for—
ARGYLL, VULCAN, SWIFT,
and
RUSTON HORNSBY CARS.

Also Agents for—
ROLLS-ROYCE,
ANGUS SANDERSON,
ROVER, & DODGE CARS.

Luxurious LANDAULETTE and TOURING CARS for Hire.

ALL CLASSES OF REPAIRS UNDERTAKEN.

Repairs to Tyres, Tubes, Etc., Undertaken
with Harvey-Frost Vulcanizing Plant. . . . .

Fully Equipped Workshop & Staff of First-Class Mechanics.

Full Stock of all Motor Accessories.

ACCUMULATORS RE-CHARGED.

Modern Motor Hearse for Hire.

Goodall's advert.

Four

Garages and Coachbuilders

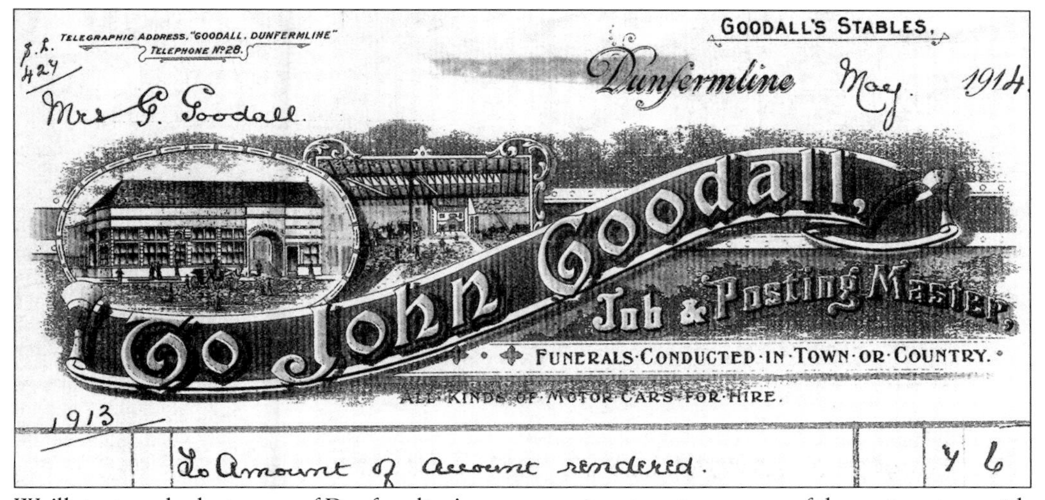
TELEGRAPHIC ADDRESS, "GOODALL, DUNFERMLINE" TELEPHONE Nº 28.

GOODALL'S STABLES,

Dunfermline May 1914

Mrs G. Goodall.

To John Goodall, Job & Posting Master,

FUNERALS·CONDUCTED·IN·TOWN·OR·COUNTRY.

ALL KINDS OF MOTOR CARS FOR HIRE.

1913	To Amount of account rendered.		4	6

We'll start our look at some of Dunfermline's more prominent motor garages of the past century with that of John Goodall & Co., whose business survived in the town for over a hundred years. Starting in 1869, when he was only seventeen years of age, John Goodall bought a horse, a cab and a set of harness at a total cost of a few pence over £23. He rented a single stall stable just off East Port, in what is now known as Commercial School Lane. As his business expanded he moved, in 1875, to larger premises at 58 Queen Anne Street, from where the Goodall family would trade for the next hundred years. In these premises Mr Goodall established a stabling and posting business which was on a par with the best in the country. He was able to supply all types of horse-drawn transport from hearses to charabancs and was regularly called upon to convey visiting dignitaries including, on several occasions, royalty. In 1910, Mr Goodall added motor limousines to his fleet and also became involved in the supply and repair of motor vehicles. The business soon acquired dealership status for a number of motor car manufacturers of the day, including for a time, Rolls-Royce – see advert on opposite page. In 1913, John Goodall retired and control of the business passed to his nephews, David Goodall and David Tullis. In 1930 the company became sole distributors of Wolseley cars for Fife and Kinross, a role they would fulfil for the next forty years. During this era Goodall also became agents for Austin, Riley, Morris and M.G. cars. In 1950, Goodall's limousine hire section closed as the firm expanded in the car sales and repair market. When David Goodall died in 1960, while still taking an active interest in the business, control fell to his son, Cameron. The company continued to play a prominent part in Dunfermline business life and remained independent until 1975, when the business was acquired by Messrs Taggarts (Motherwell) Ltd. Cameron Goodall remained in place as managing director but moved to the Fife Motor Company a year later when that firm was also bought out by Taggarts. The Queen Anne Street premises were subsequently demolished to make way for the Kingsgate Shopping Arcade. This Goodall's bill heading (above) from 1914 depicts the Queen Anne Street premises during the early part of the century.

Above is an early view of John Goodall's stables at 58 Queen Anne Street, showing the original arched entrance. To the left is one of Goodall's renowned horse-drawn cabs with uniformed driver. The advert below, from the late 1800s, highlights the various services provided by Mr Goodall at that time, with the emphasis being on the careful drivers he provided, a little different from what is suggested in Fraser & Carmichael's advert on page 4.

JOHN GOODALL,

CARRIAGE

HIRER, &c.

QUEEN ANNE STREET,
DUNFERMLINE.

THE LARGEST POSTING ESTABLISHMENT IN FIFE.

CARRIAGES, WAGGONETTES, OMNIBUSES, &c., ON HIRE.

CAREFUL DRIVERS.

FUNERALS Conducted in Town or in Country at

— MODERATE CHARGES —

Telephone, No. 728.

24

In addition to the sale and repair of motor cars, John Goodall retained a fleet of luxury limousines, which, like his horse drawn vehicles, were always maintained to the highest standard. These cars were used by many celebrities and dignitaries, including members of the royal family, whilst visiting the town. Goodall's first such vehicle was the Edwardian Daimler seen above, whilst below we see chauffeurs Jimmy McPherson and Willie Leslie with a Wolseley 25 and a Humber Pullman from the firm's war-time fleet. The shrouds fitted to the headlights of these cars were war time requirements, as were the white-painted bumpers.

The above photograph shows the interior of Goodall's premises during the 1950s with a car entering, in the background, from Queen Anne Street. In front of the petrol pumps on the left can be seen an electrically operated turn-table onto which cars would be driven and turned around, before being re-fuelled and departing by the route whence they came. The cobbles in the foreground were a relic from the horse era. Below we see Goodall's Inglis Street entrance which gave access to the workshop area. In 1960 Goodall was forced to re-develop this area, including the two adjacent buildings, to provide the premises with a purpose built filling-station after it became illegal to store large quantities of petroleum spirit inside the building.

THE FIFE MOTOR CO.,

DUNFERMLINE.

Telephone No. 124. **Telegrams: "BONNAR, DUNFERMLINE."**

Sole Agents for
"ARGYLL," "SWIFT," "VAUXHALL," & "TALBOT" CARS.
and "HALLY INDUSTRIAL" MOTORS,

MOTORISTS

Why it is to your advantage to deal with us.

We are on the spot. Should you have any trouble, we immediately send an Expert to examine your Motor at your own house, tell you what is required, and Estimate the Cost of Repair, entirely Free of Charge.

Don't incur the useless expense of sending your Car away, or getting a man from some distant town, which entails considerable delay. We can do the work quite as well in very much shorter time, and consequently at less cost.

Write, Call, or 'Phone. Lists Free on Application.

TRIAL RUNS ARRANGED.

Motor Cars for Hire by Hour, Day, Week, or Year.

Special Terms to Touring Parties.

Another of Dunfermline's prominent motor dealers of the Twentieth Century was The Fife Motor Company. Its roots can be traced back to 1901 when Peter Taylor Bonnar began selling petrol from the family ironmonger shop in the High Street. A couple of years later Mr Bonnar, under the name of The Fife Motor Company, started a motor repair workshop in Victoria Terrace, running this in conjunction with the family business. In 1910, by which time 'The Fife' held dealerships for several makes of motor vehicle, the company moved to larger premises at 12 St Margaret's Street, where they would retain a branch until 1972. In 1913 a significant move was made when 'The Fife' was appointed to sell Morris cars. The firm was to prosper from this relationship and over the years became main distributors of Morris cars and commercials throughout the Fife, Kinross and Clackmannan areas. In 1918 larger premises became available in Halbeath Road, next to East End Park, and 'The Fife' moved its main workshop there. These premises were greatly added to over the years and the business continued to flourish under the guidance of the family of Tom Gibson, who had joined the firm in 1919 as a cashier, and to whom control of the business passed on the death of Mr Bonnar in 1935. The Fife Motor Company survived until 1976 when, like Goodalls, it was bought over by the Lanarkshire based firm of Taggarts Ltd.

The entrance (above) to The Fife Motor Company premises in St Margaret Street after it was given a face-lift around 1960. These premises are now part of a night-club and discotheque. Below we see the interior of the St Margaret's Street premises before modernisation with several cars of the 1950s in the background. Like Goodalls, 'The Fife' had restricted space to manoeuvre cars and a turntable was again provided to ease the situation. This one (centre of photograph) was not electrically operated however and required to be pushed round manually by the petrol pump attendants.

Above we see the frontage of The Fife Motor Company's Halbeath Road premises, whilst below we have the firm's workshop staff from around 1950. This photograph includes (from the back): Tom Welsh;Vic Conners; Jackie Duncan; Ronnie Duncan; Jimmy Wright; Grant Gibson; Davie Hume; Tom Griffin; Ladislav Novak; Ewan Farrell; Bill Henderson and Ross Sanderson. Interestingly, at least Messrs Conners, Duncan, Duncan, Gibson, Farrell and Henderson went on to run motor trade businesses in their own right.

The All British
Standard
CARS

In either the 11 h.p. or 14 h.p. Models are recognised throughout the British Isles to be the "Standard" of RELIABILITY. This fact, coupled with the LOW PRICE and LOW RUNNING COST, makes a unique value which cannot be equalled.

Send for Latest Specification.

Trial Runs arranged.

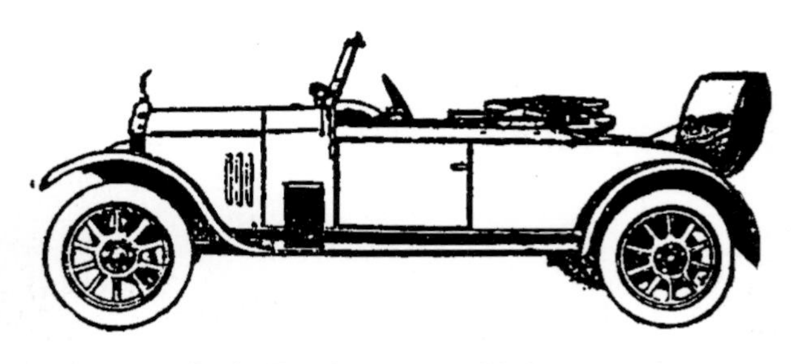

£235 (11 h.p. 2-Seater.)

11 h.p. 4-Seater, With All-Weather Body, £235.
14 h.p. 5-Seater, £375.

Other Models ranging up to Saloons at £525.

'Phone, 279.

WHITEHEAD

PRIORY LANE — REID STREET,
DUNFERMLINE.

James Whitehead was born in 1884, in Rolland Street, Dunfermline, the youngest of nine children. After leaving school at fourteen, he served his time as an engineer with Thomson of Castleblair. For a time after that he was chauffeur to Dr Tuke, a doctor of some standing in the town. During this time he saw the potential for a future in the motor trade and, in 1919, plucked up the courage to borrow £100 and started in business as motor lorry repairer, working from a shed in the garden of his home at 59 Priory Lane. As the business began to flourish a more permanent building was constructed at the rear of his home with an entrance to it from Reid Street. In these early days petrol was usually sold in two gallon tins but Mr Whitehead progressed to install two hand operated pumps dispensing R.O.P. (Russian Oil Petroleum) at his premises. The Weights and Measures Officers visited regularly to examine these pumps for accuracy. They charged for this and had an additional charge for carrying their instruments to each site. Mr Whitehead refused to pay the carriage charge and the case went to court where legal history was made and Weights and Measures were no longer allowed to levy the carriage charge. As business continued to build, a showroom was opened at the corner of Canmore Street that was used to display new cars but also sold cycles and wirelesses. On the commercial vehicle side Whitehead had been appointed agents for Chevrolet motor lorries, these being the fore-runner to the Bedford lorries with which the firm would be associated with for many years. After the war, by which time he also held the agency for Vauxhall cars, Mr Whitehead built larger premises on Nethertown Broad Street. There the business continued to expand, with fifty staff, until the early 1970s when lack of space forced another move, this time to the town's old greyhound race stadium on Milesmark Road. With six acres of ground, fronting onto one of the main roads into the town, this was an ideal site and a large showroom and workshop were built. Shortly afterwards however, the garage enterprise was sold to Curtis Motors who still operate the Vauxhall/Bedford dealership from the Milesmark site.

James Whitehead is the gentleman in the cloth cap in the centre of the above photograph of Edwardian motor cars. It must date from around the end of the first world war as the notices on the cars read, 'To the Football Match – Fare 6d – Proceeds to go to the Belgian Relief Fund'. Whitehead's Canmore Street showroom from around 1950 is shown below with two of the firm's Bedford vans parked outside. Note the display of 1950s wirelesses in the corner window.

Above shows part of Whitehead's Nethertown Broad Street premises in the 1960s whilst below is a group of the staff from the same period, probably at a works dance. The group comprises: Standing – Jim Brown, Al Mercer, Davie Day, Roy McKenzie, Eddie Riddick, Jock Anderson, Ray Harris, Jock Jamieson, Willie Wallace and Frank Sharp. Front – Frank Honeyman, Davie Wright, Tom Salmon and Sandy Gibb. Jock Anderson was workshop foreman and was with Whitehead for most of his working life, whilst Sandy Gibb was service manager for many years.

JOHN JACKSON, Carriage, Motor Body, Van and Lorry Builder,

Mill Street Coach and Joinery Works,

109 Mill Street, DUNFERMLINE

AXLES and SPRINGS, VAN and LORRY WHEELS.
GLASS SCREENS AND CAPE CART HOODS.

On leaving school John Jackson served his time as a joiner and wheelwright with Kilgour & Sons, St Leonard's Street, Dunfermline. In 1908 he acquired small premises at High Beveridgewell and started his own business, concentrating initially on the wheelwright side of his profession. He had very little capital but an abundance of enthusiasm and this, allied to his desire to turn out quality work, soon saw him secure work covering all aspects of horse-drawn and motor coach building. A move to larger premises at 109 Mill Street soon became a necessity and Mr Jackson became highly proficient at designing and building bodies for all types of commercial vehicles. At that time these vehicles would be supplied new by the manufacturer in basic chassis form and the body would be built locally to the customer's specification.

Motor bus bodies were a particular speciality with Jackson and, during the 1920s and 1930s, he built the bodywork of numerous buses owned by the many private bus operators who plied the routes throughout Fife at that time. Bus building at Mill Street proved to be a problem however as the main door to the premises was not high enough to allow the finished article to pass through. More often than not, the wheels had to be removed and the bus had to be trundled out of the building on its brake drums before the wheels could be replaced. A solution was found in 1932 when an area of ground was purchased on the north side of Pittencrieff Street and a large new workshop, with suitable doors, was erected. John Jackson had by this time been joined in the business by his sons John and William and his daughter Margaret. The business then encompassed such trades as coach-building, coach-painting, panel beating, upholstery and sign-writing.

As the firm prospered after the war John Jnr. and William took on more responsibility for the running of the business with John attending to the design work, whilst William looked after the workshop, ensuring that the quality of workmanship insisted upon by his father was maintained. During the 1950s when there was less demand for bus bodies the firm moved on to the building of travelling shops and refridgerated vans for food wholesalers. The business continued to turn out quality workmanship until 1978 when, with John Jnr and William both having reached retirement age, and having no family members wishing to carry on the business, the decision was taken to cease trading. The premises at Pittencrieff Street were not to be lost to the motor trade however, as the long established firm of Flear & Thomson, Motor Engineers, soon moved in as a result of losing their Upper Station Road premises to the new multi-storey car park development.

Above are John Jackson and family in their rather grand Sunbeam motor car outside the family home at 84 Victoria Terrace, Dunfermline. Below we see Jackson's staff around 1930 at the Mill Street workshop. From the left they are: Margaret Jackson, clerkess; Jock Campbell, machineman; John Jackson Jnr, William Jackson, John Jackson Snr, Willie Thomson, trimmer; George Fothergill, coachbuilder; Willie Slimmings, coach-painter; Willie Kay, coachbuilder; and Sandy Ramsey, foreman. Seated in front is James (?) Myles, apprentice.

These photographs from the early 1930s show the spacious main workshop of Jackson's new premises at Pittencrieff Street. The bus undergoing repairs is a 1928 Vulcan belonging to bus operator, David Clark of Glencraig. Best use was obviously made of the space available as in the photograph above the office accommodation can be seen set into the roof trusses at the rear of the workshop.

A busy scene in Jackson's well equipped woodworking machine shop (above) where the ash framing used in the construction of motor vehicle bodies was cut and shaped. The wood shavings on the floor would surely present something of a fire hazard. The scene below of Jackson's paint shop shows a Studebaker and a Crossley being spray painted and polished to Jackson's high standard. Spray painting was very much in its infancy at that time with most vehicles still being brush painted, with a finishing coat of varnish.

Another coachbuilding business in the town to survive the test of time was that of George Kay & Sons, who had premises in Inglis Street and latterly in Campbell Street. George Kay, seen here in the bowler hat, with his staff from around the turn of the century, founded the business in 1881. He specialised in horse drawn transport and indeed when the motor car made an appearance he resisted the temptation to have anything to do with 'these new-fangled contraptions' claiming they would be 'just be a flash in the pan'.

Notwithstanding George Kay's apparent dislike of the motor car he did get involved in what might have been the only vintage car to be built in the town. The Tod three-wheeler was the product of Micheal Tod's Engineering Works in Campbell Street, who carried out the mechanical work and Mr Kay, who constructed the bodywork. Unfortunately the car did not progress beyond the prototype stage, so this particular one probably was 'just a flash in the pan'.

In this line up of Kay's staff from the middle 1920s George Kay has changed his headgear and is joined by his sons, Dick (extreme right) and Jimmy (second right). Dick succeeded his father in controlling the firm and was apparently an excellent coach-painter, having the somewhat dubious reputation of regularly applying the finishing coat of varnish to vehicles whilst in the nude, lest fibres from his clothing might contaminate the finished article.

Into the 1950s now and a new man is at the helm. Dick Kay's son George, seen here on the left, took over the management of the firm in 1937. Dick, with the bonnet on the right, remained an active member of staff and was still undertaking sign-writing work whilst in his eighties. Even in his nineties he still made the daily walk from his home in John Street, up the New Row, in order to keep an eye on things at Inglis Street. In 1975 the firm moved to new premises in Campbell Street where business was conducted until its closure in 1996.

No look at road transport in Dunfermline in the twentieth century would be complete without making mention of Willie MacFarlane. Born in Bo'ness in 1910, Willie served an engineering apprenticeship with Fife County Council, at the Milemark Depot, before starting his own business in the yard behind his grandmother's house (above) in Pittencrieff Street. His passion for steam powered vehicles probably stemmed from his days at Milesmark and was to remain with him as these photographs of his yard from around 1950 appear to imply.

An atmospheric scene is created in the High Street in the 1950s as Willie MacFarlane takes his 1924 Foden for a spin around the streets. The gent on the ladder repairing Hepworth's shop sign looks a wee bit apprehensive and no doubt the environmentalists of today would take a rather dim view of the whole situation.

Vintage cars also played a part in Willie's life and here we see him working on his *c.*1910 Fiat, which was formerly owned for many years by Captain Smith-Sligo of Inzievar Estate, Oakley. Willie's workshop looks a little bit cluttered but he always maintained that he knew where everything was, even when it took him wee while to find things.

As an aside from his engineering enterprises Willie MacFarlane also collected pre-war Rolls-Royce motor cars. In the 1950s and 1960s these cars could be bought relatively cheaply and the entrepreneur in Willie meant he did not lose sight of the fact our American cousins were willing to pay good money for them. Suffice to say that throughout his lifetime Willie owned around sixty-one Rolls-Royces, many of which finished up with new owners in the States.

This was Willie MacFarlane's yard, as most people will remember it from the 1960s, when it was a mecca for the do-it-yourself motorist seeking second-hand parts to enable his or her car to pass the then recently introduced M.O.T. test. The yard closed in 1980 when Willie retired and that area of Pittencrieff Street was re-developed.

Next door to Willie MacFarlane's yard in Pittencrieff Street in the 1950s was Angus Campbell's motor cycle repair shop. Angus, who it will be seen was then an agent for Ariel, B.S.A. and A.J.S. motor cycles, also sold pedal cycles and was reputed to be able to sell a bicycle a day and a motor cycle a week. He later moved to larger premises in Campbell Street where he became one of the largest motor cycle dealers in the area.

Around the corner from Pittencrieff Street, in Chalmers Street, were the premises of Normand & Thomson, Motor Engineers and Brassfounders. This scene shows the garage frontage from the late 1920s with a Humber 15/40 in the foreground and what appears to be a Belsize tourer behind. Although no longer in the motor trade Normand and Thomson are still in business and are still highly regarded brassfounders and coppersmiths.

Five

Blue Lights, Bikes and a Caravan

The emergency services in Dunfermline appear to have been slow to invest in motorised transport with horse drawn fire engines, ambulances and prison wagons still being the order of the day until well into the early part of the century. The police in fact did not operate a motor car in the town until the 1930s, relying until then mainly on motor cycles and pedal cycles. Handcarts or barrows were retained at police stations for conveying drunks to the cells and even this form of transport was not without it's problems, as a Kincardine constable found to his cost. One Sunday morning around 1898 he was conveying an inebriated individual through the village to the police station just as the congregation was leaving church. As a result of this apparently sacrilegious act he was reported to his Chief Constable and was duly reprimanded. The use of pedal cycles in the early days was also occasionally frowned upon as was the case when another Kincardine constable, probably showing good initiative, used his own cycle to make the 10 mile journey from Kincardine to Dunfermline in order to uplift the station wages. On arrival at Dunfermline he was spotted by an Inspector, who branded him a lazy individual for not making the journey on foot. In the photograph above, taken in 1902 on Halbeath Road where the junction with Garvockhill is now, we see members of Dunfermline City Fire Brigade lined up with a horse drawn fire pump. In those days the Fire Station was in Campbell Street and, on receipt of a fire call, a team of John Goodall's horses would be despatched from the stables in Queen Anne Street to Campbell Street. There they would be hitched up to the fire pump, the firemen would climb aboard, and 'soon' all would be on their merry way to the scene of the fire.

Dunfermline's first motorised fire engine was this purpose built Leyland unit, bought by the Town Council in 1916, and seen above in Appin Crescent in the 1930s, probably at a hospital charity event. It was capable of 35mph and would obviously provide a much faster response than its horse drawn predecessor. However, there was still a problem as the unit could not enter the Fire Station (seen below) in Campbell Street without first having the ladders removed from it. The ladders then had to be replaced each time the fire engine left the station, so perhaps the response time to a fire call was not as speedy as might have been anticipated.

Fire Tender No.3 (a Bedford 12 horse-power van), with a war time Tangye auxiliary fire pump in tow, ready to set off to the scene of a fire. The above photograph was taken shortly after the City of Dunfermline Fire Brigade moved from Campbell Street to the new fire station in Carnegie Street (now Carnegie Drive).

Probably the first motorised ambulance in Dunfermline, this 1920s Commer was attached to the West of Fife Infectious Diseases Hospital at Milesmark. A nurse from the hospital would accompany the driver to assist with patients – no paramedics in those days.

Dunfermline's first police patrol car, a 1934 Austin 16/6, photographed in Comely Park with its crew, Constables Jim Scott and Hector Law, both members of Dunfermline City Police. This was prior to the amalgamation, in 1949, of Dunfermline City Police, Kirkcaldy Burgh Police and Fife County Police.

Around 1950 and members of the recently formed Fife Constabulary's traffic department line up with a Wolseley 18/25 and a more modern Wolseley 6/80. The 6/80 was a popular vehicle with police forces throughout the country. From left to right the officers are: Constables David Watt and Ronnie Munro, Inspector William Pringle, and Constables David Martin and Jimmy Bell.

In October, 1967, a new style of policing was introduced to the streets of Fife, with the arrival of Panda Cars. Four of the Ford Anglias seen here were destined for Dunfermline. The total cost of these nine cars was under £7,000. The officers on parade are Sergeant Jim Burns, Constables Jack Brunton, Jimmy Gray, Gus Black, Dave Baillie, Willie Paton, Jim Wyllie, Harry Gray and Jock Ewan.

It is 1973 and the location is the frontage of the recently opened Police Station at Holyrood Place, with traffic officers Alan Gibb and Duncan McMillan, alongside their Triumph 2.5 patrol car. The new station superseded the cramped and long outdated accommodation at Abbey Park Place, and the Victorian cell block in the Kirkgate.

Dunfermline Motor Cycle Club members assemble in front of Wilson and Wightman's factory in Pilmuir Street for the first run of the 1949 season. Left to right are: Charlie Seaman, Tommy Niven, Charlie and Jessie Purves, Dougie and Margaret Campbell, Eric Shepherd, Vic Conners, Ian Cook, Tom Perry, Tom McNeill, and Peter and Mrs Simpson.

One form of wheeled transport no longer seen is the message bike. Most self-respecting shopkeepers of the early and middle part of the century employed youngsters to make deliveries to their customers with this form of transport. In this photograph the young man is Bert Sharp, seen here in the 1930s with his sister, Bessie, outside the family fish shop in Chalmers Street. This business would later move to a more central location in the High Street.

And lastly the story of the garden shed that thought it was a caravan. From 1907 to 1970 father and son, Will and Bert Spence, ran a carriers business from their home in Culross. Initially using a horse and cart Will delivered parcels around West Fife. This progressed to house removals and also the delivery of furnishings, etc. from shops in Dunfermline and Kirkcaldy. In the 1920s a Model T Ford lorry was acquired and for many years thereafter the Spence family took their one week trades holiday and went of to camp at Crieff. Mr Spence had built a garden shed which could be fitted onto the lorry (see above) and this served as holiday accommodation for the ladies whilst the menfolk slept in a tent. Once the holiday was over the shed reverted to its primary role (below) in the garden at Culross. No mean task each year but being in the removal business the Spence team probably had it all down to a fine art.

Sole Maker

OF THE

OELEBRATED

Dundonnachie Cycles.

HUGH ROBERTSON,

Cycle Manufacturer,

NORTH STATION ROAD,

DUNFERMLINE

SOLE AGENT FOR

Raglan, Rover, Centaur, and Triumph Cycles.

We make a Speciality of REPAIRS, and those entrusted to our care receive Careful and Prompt Attention.

Official Repairer to C.T.C.

A FULL LIST

OF THE

LATEST

Accessories and Novelties

ALWAYS IN STOCK.

Hugh Robertson advert.